A Note to Parents

DK READERS is a compelling program for beginning readers, designed in conjunction with leading literacy experts, including Dr. Linda Gambrell, Director of the School of Education at Clemson University. Dr. Gambrell has served on the Board of Directors of the International Reading Association and as President of the National Reading Conference.

Beautiful illustrations and superb full-color photographs combine with engaging, easy-to-read stories to offer a fresh approach to each subject in the series. Each DK READER is guaranteed to capture a child's interest while developing his or her reading skills, general knowledge, and love of reading.

The five levels of DK READERS are aimed at different reading abilities, enabling you to choose the books that are exactly right for your child:
Pre-level 1: Learning to read
Level 1: Beginning to read
Level 2: Beginning to read alone
Level 3: Reading alone
Level 4: Proficient readers

The "normal" age at which a child begins to read can be anywhere from three to eight years old, so these levels are only a general guideline.

No matter which level you select, you can be sure that you are helping your child learn to read, then read to learn!

LONDON, NEW YORK, MUNICH,
MELBOURNE, and DELHI

Publisher Andrew Berkhut
Editor Regina Kahney
Art Director Tina Vaughan

Reading Consultant
Linda Gambrell, Ph.D.

Produced by
NFL Publishing Group
Editorial Director John Wiebusch
Managing Editor John Fawaz
Art Director Bill Madrid

First American Edition, 2001
01 02 03 04 05 10 9 8 7 6 5 4 3 2 1
Published in the United States by DK Publishing, Inc.
375 Hudson Street, New York, New York 10014

ISBN 0-7894-7886-2 (PB)
ISBN 0-7894-7885-4 (PLC)

Color reproduction by Hong Kong Scanner.
Printed and bound in China by L Rex Printing Co., Ltd.

A Catalog Record is available from the Library of Congress.

Photography credits:
t=top, b=below, l=left, r=right, c=center.
All photos copyright NFL Photos (except *)
and these photographers.
Tom Albert: 29t; John Biever: 20; Michael Burr/NFLP: 33br;
Courtesy Chicago Bears: 21t; Merv Corning: 22; Greg Crisp: 4b;
Joe Culliton: 39t; Bruce Dierdorf: 28b; Dorling Kindersley: 13c*;
David Drapkin: 45t; Malcolm Emmons: 26b; Mitchell Friedman:
19b; Jerry Gallegos: 34, 38; Joycelyn Hinsen: 28t; Jackson State:
19t; Paul Jasienski: 5, 27br; Allen Kee: 40, 43b, 45b, 46(2), 47b,
48, 49; G. Newman Lowrance: cover br, 42r; Michael Martin:
cover bl; Al Messerschmidt: cover cr; Peter Read Miller: 27t;
Marty Morrow: 41; Layne Murdoch: 33cl; Peter Murdock: 23b;
NFL Photos: 6b, 7t, 8(2), 9t, 11t, 13tl, 26t, 33tr, 37t; Al Pereira:
43t; Evan Pinkus: 44t; Joe Poellot: 39b; Pro Football Hall of
Fame: 9b, 10, 17t; Louis Raynor: 25; Mitchell Reibel: 37cl; Frank
Rippon: 11b, 14tl; G. Robargo: 44b; Bob Rosato: 24, 36; Manny
Rubio: 21b; Todd Rosenberg: 37cr; James D. Smith: 31; Smith
Family/NFLP: 30; Chuck Solomon: 32t; Damien Strohmeyer: 18;
Syracuse University/NFLP: 12t; Kevin Terrell/NFLP: 4t, 20bl;
Tony Tomsic: 3, 6t, 12b, 15, 16, 17b; Corky Trewin: 23t; Jim
Turner: 32b; *United Press: 7b*; Ron Vesely: 2, 35, 42; Ralph
Waclawicz: 47t.
All other images © Dorling Kindersley Limited
For further information see: www.dkimages.com

Discover more at
www.dk.com

Contents

DK **READERS**

PROFICIENT
4
READERS

RUMBLING
RUNNING
BACKS

Written by James Buckley, Jr.

DK
DK Publishing, Inc.

Ground game

With just seconds to go in the big game, the home team is only two yards from a winning touchdown. But those are two tough yards. The visitors are rough, tough, and big, and will do anything to stop their opponents.

The crowd is screaming as the two teams set up at the line of scrimmage for the final play. The quarterback barks out the signals.

Who will get the ball?

At the snap, the quarterback spins and slaps the ball into the running back's belly. And then the running back is off as if he's shot from a cannon, straight into the teeth of a literal ton of angry defenders.

But he churns and he drives and powers his way through a tiny crack and dives into the end zone to score a touchdown!

Scoring
When a player carries the ball over the goal line (or catches it in the end zone), he earns his team a touchdown, worth six points.

Official ball
The official Wilson NFL football is just under a foot long and contains about 13 pounds of air pressure.

Many of football's greatest stars have been running backs, from the sport's earliest days.

They use skills that include speed, strength, agility, and field sense to make short scores or break off long, twisting touchdown runs.

In this book, you will read about the best running backs in NFL history.

Cloud of dust

In the early days of the NFL, the game was played on the ground. There were few, if any, of the long passes that are a regular part of every NFL game today.

Strategy in the early days was run, run, run...and then run some more. A popular saying was that football plays were "three yards and a cloud of dust," caused by the pile of tacklers on the ball carrier.

In this game, the running back was key. Sometimes the position was known as halfback, wingback, or fullback, but the job was the same: Take the ball and run, run, run.

The first superstar running back in the NFL was a speedy player from Illinois named Harold Grange. Everyone just called him "Red."

Red Grange helped turn the NFL from a small league with few fans into the national sport it is today.

Ouch
Early NFL players didn't wear helmets. The first helmets were flimsy leather models such as the one shown here.

Poster boy
Grange was so popular that he starred in several movies when he wasn't scoring touchdowns.

Grange joined the Chicago Bears in 1925, the NFL's sixth season, and his amazing long runs brought out record crowds. The "Galloping Ghost," as he was known, thrilled fans and created an exciting style of football.

Awesome Eskimo
Ernie Nevers was another great back of Grange's day. Nevers played for the Chicago Cardinals and Duluth Eskimos. He set a single-game mark in 1929 when he scored 40 points, a record that still stands.

More than 75 years after he entered the NFL, Red Grange remains one of the league's greatest heroes.

Grange suffered a knee injury in 1928, and wasn't the same after that. But another player from his era was also an all-time great runner, with a great name for a football player—Bronko Nagurski.

Bronko lived up to his bruising name. The big running back from Minnesota was nearly impossible to tackle. He joined the Chicago Bears in 1930 after a great college career at the University of Minnesota.

One tackler told of giving Bronko the hardest hit he could and thinking he had stopped the big back. He had—eight yards from where he first ran into him!

Along with being a powerful runner, Bronko was one of the game's best blockers, a great defensive player (he was a linebacker on defense), and a good passer. He threw touchdown

passes in two of the championship games he helped the Bears win in the 1930s.

Nagurski carved out a legend of football toughness and power that has never been topped.

Grange and Nagurski both were members of the first class of the Pro Football Hall of Fame in 1963.

Two-way players
In the early days of football, most players played both offense and defense. For instance, Nagurski was a powerful linebacker.

Powerful runner
Marion Motley helped redefine running by using his awesome power simply to run over defenders. He was as great at tackling on defense as he was at running on offense, and he helped the Browns win the 1950 NFL title.

The forward pass became a much bigger part of a football team's strategy during the 1940s. However, powerful running backs still were an important part of the game.

One of the best of the decade was Steve Van Buren of the Philadelphia Eagles.

"When Steve carried the ball, he struck fear in the hearts of the defense," said Eagles teammate Russ Craft. "He ran so hard, you could see the dirt flying off his cleats. When he hit the line, he looked like a bulldozer going through a picket fence."

Van Buren helped the Eagles win NFL titles in 1948 and 1949 and twice gained more than 1,000 yards in a season, even though NFL teams played only 12 games a season then.

Van Buren, a big man at more than 200 pounds, was also one of the fastest men in the league.

Teammate Clyde Scott was an Olympic hurdler, but Van Buren could beat Scott in a 40-yard dash.

Van Buren still holds the Eagles' records for most rushing yards in a game, and most touchdowns in a season and a career.

More great running backs followed as pro football became the nation's favorite sport.

Van Buren scored the only touchdown in Philadelphia's 7-0 victory in the 1948 NFL title game, played in a blizzard.

The best ever?

"Trying to tackle Jim Brown," moaned one defender, "is like trying to tackle a runaway freight train."

That mighty train chugged through the NFL for nine amazing seasons from 1957-1965. In that time, Brown won eight NFL rushing titles, set NFL records that stood for decades, and created a career that

Jim Brown combined speed, strength, and great moves with a fierce determination never to be stopped.

some call the greatest in NFL history...at any position.

Jim Brown was born in Georgia and grew up on Long Island, New York. He was a great athlete in every sport he tried. He was all-state in football, track, lacrosse [la-CROSS], and basketball. He once scored 55 points in a high school hoops game.

He attended college at Syracuse University in central New York. Again, he starred in many sports.

Along with excelling at track and basketball, Brown also became one of the greatest lacrosse players in the history of that sport.

But football was where he made his lasting mark.

He did it all
This is a stick used in lacrosse to toss a ball back and forth down the field before throwing it toward a goal. It is a hard-hitting game of speed and skill.

On track
Brown's great athletic skills showed in the decathlon, where athletes compete in 10 track and field events. He was fifth in the nation as a college sophomore.

NFL draft
NFL teams choose college players at this event, held each April in New York City.

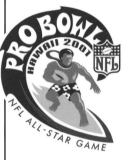

Pro Bowl
This is the NFL's All-Star game, held every February in Hawaii. The contest matches All-Stars from the American Football Conference and the National Football Conference.

At Syracuse, Brown pounded opposing defenses game after game. He was chosen by the Cleveland Browns with the sixth pick of the first round of the 1957 NFL draft.

As a rookie in 1957, Brown led the NFL with 942 rushing yards and 9 touchdowns. He quickly established an unmatched reputation for toughness, even in a tough game such as football.

In nine seasons, Brown never missed a game because of an injury. He simply refused to come out of the game, even if he was hurt. That's very impressive for a star player who was the target of every defense he played against.

Brown was named the league's rookie of the year and most valuable player in 1957 and earned the first of his nine Pro Bowl selections.

Brown only got better, winning NFL rushing titles in each of the next four seasons. In 1958, he set a single-season record with 17 rushing touchdowns.

Weather or not
In Jim Brown's day, just like today, NFL games go on regardless of the weather. While on the sidelines, players wear capes or coats to keep warm and dry, as Brown did here.

Fellow star
Another star
halfback during
Jim Brown's era
was Lenny
Moore of the
Baltimore
Colts. Using
more speed
than power, he
scored 113
touchdowns in
12 seasons.

Score!
Brown (32),
scores 1 of his
126 career
touchdowns,
the fourth-
highest total
ever.

Believe it or not, Jim Brown got even better. In 1963, he rushed for 1,863 yards, a single-season record that stood for 10 years.

The great linebacker Sam Huff was once asked how to stop Brown.

"Easy," Huff answered. "Don't let him leave the locker room."

In 1965, Brown again ran for 17 touchdowns, led the league in rushing, and was as unstoppable as ever. But then he proved that the only person who could stop Jim Brown was himself.

At the age of 30, he suddenly retired from football. Cleveland Browns fans were stunned, as were teammates and coaches. Brown was going his own way, just like always.

Jim Brown became an actor in movies and later worked as a community leader to end gang violence.

Brown the hero
Six years after his final game, Jim Brown was elected to the Pro Football Hall of Fame in his first year of eligibility.

Jim Brown's rushing totals remain among the best ever, more than 30 years after he finished.

But the numbers don't tell the whole Jim Brown story. That story is written by the admiration of the defenses that tried to stop him...and the NFL fans who loved to watch him play.

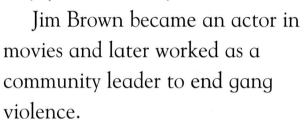

Old town team
The Chicago Bears are one of the NFL's original teams. They began play as the Decatur Staleys in 1920.

Online football
Payton's fans voted for him on NFL.com, the official Website of the NFL. The site also has a special kids' area called "Play Football."

Sweetness

Hundreds of great athletes have played running back in the NFL. But none have run for more yards—or earned the love and respect of more fans—than Walter Payton of the Chicago Bears.

Fans voting on NFL.com during the 1999 season named Payton the "greatest player of the century." There is a lot of evidence that they made the right choice.

Payton ran for 16,726 yards, more than any other player. He set the single-game rushing record (since broken) with an amazing 275-yard performance in a 1977 victory over Minnesota.

He is among the leaders in rushing touchdowns with 110. And he did it all for Bears teams that weren't strong early in his career.

Payton played college football at Jackson State in Mississippi.

After setting numerous school records, he was the Bears' first-round pick in the 1975 NFL draft.

In 1977, only his third season, he led the NFL with 1,852 rushing yards and 16 total touchdowns.

College kid
Payton played four years at Jackson State, becoming the school's all-time leading rusher with 3,563 yards, and he also scored 66 touchdowns.

Papa Bear
George Halas, who owned the Bears when they drafted Payton, was a part of the Bears for more than 60 years.

Backfield blocking
On pass plays, running backs often have to block blitzing linebackers. Payton excelled at doing that.

In the flat
Most pass plays to running backs are for short yardage, usually to the side, called "in the flat."

Payton quickly gained a reputation as one of the game's best all-around players. Not only could he run—either around you or over you—but he was a great receiver and a powerful blocker.

"In the middle of a game, you'd come to the sideline and say, 'Did you see what he did?'" said former NFL linebacker Matt Millen.

Payton combined the ability to power for short yardage or race around end for a long gain.

Perhaps more important, he earned a reputation as one of the nicest men to play the game.

The Bears slowly improved around Payton. In 1984, they played in the NFC Championship Game. Chicago lost, but the stage was set for a big year in 1985.

The Bears were a powerful team on both offense and defense that season. Payton ran for 1,551 yards. The Bears' defense was one of the best in NFL history. Super Bowl XX seemed like the only place they could end up.

And that's where they went. With Payton leading the way, the Bears crushed the New England Patriots 46-10 for the team's ninth NFL championship.

Payton ran for a game-high 61 yards in Super Bowl XX, helping to power the Bears to a 46-10 victory.

Singing Bears
Midway through the 1985 season, several Bears, including Payton, recorded a song called the "Super Bowl Shuffle."

The first title
The Chicago Bears (then called the Chicago Staleys) won their first championship in 1921, the second year of the league's existence.

The coach
"He was the best football player I've ever seen," said former Bears coach Mike Ditka. "And one of the best people I ever met."

After the Super Bowl triumph, Payton played two more seasons. When he retired in 1987, he was the NFL's all-time leader in rushing yards. He had been named to nine Pro Bowls. He had rushed for at least 1,000 yards in 10 seasons.

In 1993, he was elected to the Pro Football Hall of Fame. In 1994, he was named to the NFL's 75th Anniversary All-Time Team.

And he enjoyed a business career that was as successful as his football career.

Then, in 1999, Walter Payton got sick. The man who was so tough that he had started a club-record 184 consecutive games was stricken with a rare form of liver disease.

American sports fans were saddened by his illness, but were inspired by his courage and his love for life. Payton and his family battled together, but in November, 1999, liver cancer took his life at the age of 45.

Payton remains an NFL legend, as much for what he did on the field as what he did after leaving it.

His nickname was perfect. They called him "Sweetness."

Thanks, Walter
In 1999, the NFL's annual award to a player who excels on the field and in the community was renamed the Walter Payton Award.

The son
When Walter Payton was inducted into the Pro Football Hall of Fame in 1993, his son, Jarrett, then 12, gave a speech welcoming his father into the Hall. "He's my role model," Jarrett said.

He made 'em miss

I've got him, thought dozens of NFL linebackers during Barry Sanders's career. I've got him right where I want him. He's coming right at me, full speed ahead. I can make the tackle, no problem.

And then suddenly, poof, Sanders wasn't there. And the defender was left grabbing air instead of Barry.

The Detroit Lions' running back had an incredible ability to cut on a dime, to twist and turn and swerve and make defenders miss.

"He makes you miss tackles so bad, you look up in the stands to see if anyone was watching you," Atlanta defensive back D.J. Johnson once said.

The shifty, speedy Sanders devastated defenses for 10 seasons. He won four NFL rushing titles and is the only player to have five seasons with 1,500 or more rushing yards.

Sanders ran for 15,269 yards, the second-most yards in NFL history, and gained most of them by magically avoiding the grasp of football's best defenders.

All-Star
Barry was selected to the Pro Bowl after each of his 10 seasons in the NFL.

More numbers
Sanders ran for 150 or more yards in 25 games, the most ever. He also had 15 touchdown runs of 50 or more yards.

Sanders played college football at Oklahoma State. In three years there, he set 13 national records, including a stunning 2,628 yards as a junior in 1988. That year, he won the Heisman Trophy.

With all that success, Sanders chose to leave college and turn pro. The Lions were glad that he did.

In his rookie season, Sanders set franchise records with 1,470 yards and 14 touchdowns. In his second season, he won the NFL rushing title. In 1991, his third season, he led the league with 17 touchdowns and was second with 1,548 rushing yards.

Those are amazing numbers, but what set Sanders apart was how he piled those numbers up. Some of his escapes from tacklers were almost magical. If one side of the line was crowded, no problem. He just stopped suddenly, switched gears, and ran to the other side.

Sometimes he would run 40 yards back and forth across the field just to gain 5 yards.

"He's the most fun player in the league to watch," said Marcus Allen. "And the most dangerous."

Super Sims
Billy Sims was another top Lions running back. But Barry Sanders came along and broke all of his club records.

Awesome Allen
In 16 seasons with the Raiders and Chiefs, Marcus Allen ran for 123 touchdowns, the second-highest total ever. Barry Sanders ran for 99 scores.

Sanders kept piling up the yards throughout the 1990s. He won rushing titles in 1994 and 1996. He kept making people miss. He kept making fans ooh and ahh!

In 1997, Sanders had his best season in the NFL.

The first 2,000
In 1973, O.J. Simpson of the Buffalo Bills became the first player to run for 2,000 yards in one season, gaining 2,003. Since then, Eric Dickerson, Barry Sanders, and Terrell Davis have topped 2,000 yards.

Did you know?
Barry Sanders wore number 20. All NFL running backs wear numbers from 20-49, except in rare cases.

With 2,053 rushing yards, he became only the third player to reach 2,000 yards in one season.

When reporters asked

him after the game how he felt, the first thing he did was thank his offensive line.

"No running back can succeed without their help," he said.

Barry was named the league's co-most valuable player while setting a record for most 100-yard games (14) in a season. He moved to second place on the league's all-time rushing yards list.

He was on the way to perhaps the greatest career ever for a running back.

Then, suddenly, before the 1999 season, he decided to retire.

His teammates and coaches were stunned, but they weren't the only ones. Like so many would-be tacklers, Lions fans now miss Sanders, too.

Record setter
Barry was greeted by his father after the final game of 1997, in which Sanders topped the 2,000-yard mark.

Going long
In 1997, Sanders became the first player in history to score 3 touchdowns of more than 80 yards in one season, including 2 in one game!

80+

Scoring machine

Wherever he has played, Emmitt Smith has broken records...along with hundreds of tackles. A strong, durable runner with speed, Smith has become one of the NFL's most popular players.

Smith started breaking records in his native Florida. At Escambia High School in Pensacola, he ran for the third-most yards in national high school history. The newspaper *USA Today* named Smith the player of the year.

Many colleges wanted Smith to play for them, but he decided to stay in his home state.

Big D
The Dallas Cowboys joined the NFL in 1960. The team has played in eight Super Bowls, the most ever, and has won five of them.

Emmitt was one of the best high school runners ever.

At the University of Florida, he quickly made his mark. In his first start, he set a school record with 224 yards. Two years later, he ran for 316 yards in a game, and he went on to set Florida records for most yards in a season and in a career.

After his junior year, Smith chose to move on to the NFL.

The Dallas Cowboys chose him with the seventeenth pick in the NFL draft. Just as in high school and college, he wasted no time making his mark. Smith led NFL rookies with 11 touchdowns and earned rookie of the year honors. It was the first of his many awards.

Fellow Cowboy Emmitt Smith and quarterback Troy Aikman form one of the NFL's great duos. Together, they have helped the Cowboys win three Super Bowls.

The old record
In 1995, Smith's record of 25 touchdowns topped the mark of 24, set in 1983 by John Riggins of the Redskins.

Fumble
When a player drops the ball while running with it, it is called a fumble. Either team can recover it once it's out of the player's control.

During the next five years, Smith compiled some amazing seasons:

• 1991: Earned his first NFL rushing title, the first Dallas player to do so.

• 1992: Set a Cowboys' record with 1,713 yards. Won NFL rushing title again.

• 1993: While winning third NFL rushing title, was named league most valuable player.

• 1994: Led NFL with 22 touchdowns; did not fumble once in 418 chances.

• 1995: Set NFL record (since broken) with 25 touchdowns while winning fourth rushing title.

Those are great numbers indeed, but more important, Smith helped the Cowboys win three Super Bowls during that time.

In Super Bowl XXVII, Dallas defeated Buffalo 52-17. Smith ran for 108 yards and 1 touchdown.

In Super Bowl XXVIII, Smith ran for 132 yards and 2 touchdowns to earn the game's MVP award, as Dallas beat the Bills 30-13.

Smith rushed for 5 touchdowns in the Cowboys' three Super Bowl victories.

Star for Smith
Smith earned this Pete Rozelle Trophy for being the MVP in Super Bowl XXVIII. Rozelle was the NFL's long-time commissioner.

Super silver
The Cowboys have won the Vince Lombardi Trophy five times. The award, which goes to the Super Bowl champion, is named for legendary Green Bay Packers coach Vince Lombardi.

Dallas capped its "Super" run with a victory in Super Bowl XXX. Smith again scored 2 touchdowns as the Cowboys beat the Steelers 27-17 for their third title in four seasons.

Smith's success

Super score
Here's Smith scoring in Super Bowl XXX. His 5 rushing touchdowns are a Super Bowl career record.

TD king
San Francisco wide receiver Jerry Rice is the NFL's all-time leader in touchdowns, with more than 180 in his amazing career.

continues. In 2000, he became only the second player to rush for 1,000 yards in 10 consecutive seasons (Barry Sanders was the first). Smith is now third all time in rushing yards behind Walter Payton and Sanders.

If the object of the game is to score touchdowns, then Emmitt Smith is the best running back ever. He is the all-time leader in rushing touchdowns, and he trails only Jerry Rice in total touchdowns.

And if he ever needs inspiration to keep going, all he has to do is go to a special room in his house.

There he can see every football he has ever scored with, from college to the pros. Smith doesn't spike them, he just carries them off the field...another souvenir of a great career, another six points for the Cowboys, and another mark in his amazing record book.

Spike
Smith usually doesn't do this, but some players slam, or spike, the ball into the ground after they score.

Go, man, go!
"It's been a tremendous ride," Smith says. "And the ride is not over. I've got young legs. I hope the best is yet to come."

Early days

Davis grew up in San Diego, California. After his father died at a young age, Davis and his four brothers were raised by his mother, Kateree.

Bulldog days

After one season at California's Long Beach State, Davis moved across the nation to attend the University of Georgia.

Just call him T.D.

Players who are drafted in the sixth round of the NFL draft are not expected to be stars. Most just hope they can make the team, play as a backup, perhaps get a few starts. They're good players, not superstars.

Terrell Davis was an exception.

Denver selected Davis in the sixth round of the 1995 draft after he had a quiet college career at the University of Georgia. As it turned out, the Broncos had found an unexpected star.

Davis earned the starting job as a rookie and quickly showed that the teams that had passed on him had made a big mistake.

He gained 1,117 yards, becoming the lowest-drafted rookie ever to gain 1,000 yards. He showed the power, speed, and drive that would make him one of the best running backs in the game.

In 1996, he set a club record with 1,538 yards, leading the AFC in rushing. He was named the NFL MVP by *Sports Illustrated*, and earned a spot in the Pro Bowl.

Mile-high team Mile High Stadium, the Broncos' home from 1960-2000, got its name because Denver is a mile above sea level.

From the defense "Terrell Davis is like the Energizer Bunny," says safety LeRoy Butler. "He just keeps going and going and going."

Wild card
An NFL team that doesn't win its division, but has a record good enough to make the playoffs, is called a "wild-card" team.

Oh, my head
When Davis suffers a migraine headache, his vision blurs, his head throbs, and he has pain in the front of his head. Rest and medicine can ease his symptoms.

In 1997, Davis continued his success, this time joined by the rest of the team. The Broncos earned a wild-card playoff spot by finishing second in the AFC West.

In three playoff games, Davis scored 5 touchdowns, helping the Broncos earn a spot in Super Bowl XXXII. There, Davis showed both his strength and courage.

Since he was a kid, Davis had suffered from painful migraine [MY-grain] headaches. Suddenly, in the first half of his biggest game, he had one. He had to leave the game to recover.

But he knew his team needed him, so he returned in the second half. Davis ran for 157 yards and a Super Bowl-record 3 touchdowns to help Denver defeat the Green Bay Packers 31-24. He was named the Super Bowl XXXII most valuable player.

Not bad for a sixth-round draft pick whom few expected to succeed.

He was even better in 1998. Davis ran for 2,008 yards and scored 23 touchdowns. The Broncos won Super Bowl XXXIII in quarterback John Elway's last game.

Although he missed most of the 1999 and 2000 seasons because of injuries, Davis remains one of the NFL's best running backs.

Top Bronco
John Elway teamed with Terrell Davis to lead the Broncos to two titles. Elway is among the best quarterbacks in NFL history.

How he does it
"It's hard to explain," Davis says. "It's seeing the field and knowing what the defense is going to do before they do it. You don't have time to think, you just do it."

Indiana home
The Colts have played in Indianapolis since 1984, when they moved from Baltimore.

Hurricane James
Edgerrin was one of the nation's best running backs at Miami.

Indy's "Edge"

After what Colts' runner Edgerrin [EDGE-er-in] James went through growing up, dodging NFL defensive players must seem easy.

James grew up in a tough, rural neighborhood in southwest Florida. James lived in a one-room apartment with his mother and four brothers and sisters. His family relied on food stamps and their mother's hard work, and Christmas wasn't always celebrated.

But Edgerrin knew that he could make it, thanks to his determination and his athletic skills. He just had to use them the right way.

Edgerrin has a saying taped to his computer: "Adversity [which means having obstacles to overcome] causes some people to break."

But it goes on to say, "Adversity causes other people to break records."

Edgerrin is one of the "other people" in that saying.

He broke several records at Miami, becoming the first player at the school to run for 1,000 yards in two different seasons.

In 1999, Indianapolis chose Edgerrin with the fourth overall pick in the NFL draft.

In his first season in the NFL, the records kept falling.

Young star
James's teammate, Peyton Manning, earned Pro Bowl selections in each of his first two seasons.

Practice, practice
The Colts' great trio of players does well in games because they give their all in practice. "If you practice hard, it makes the games easy," James says.

James had one of the best rookie seasons in NFL history. He led the NFL with a club-record 1,553 rushing yards. He was the first rookie to lead the league since Eric Dickerson in 1983. His 10 100-yard games were the most ever for a first-year player.

On the Colts, James teamed with quarterback Peyton Manning and wide receiver Marvin Harrison to form one of the NFL's best young trios of players.

The team lost 13 games in 1998. After James joined the Colts, they *won* 13 games. It was the best one-season turnaround in NFL history.

James is one of the most highly regarded players in the NFL. He is a powerful, fast runner, and an excellent pass receiver. He was second on the team in 1999 with 62 receptions. He finished the year as the youngest player in history to gain more than 2,000 combined yards rushing and receiving in a season.

"There aren't too many backs out there who are faster than me," James says. "Or can catch like me. Or can make moves like me."

That's not bragging…that's just telling the truth.

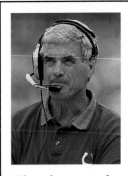

Thanks, coach
"Edgerrin can be going one way and—bam—he'll plant his foot and go the other," says Colts coach Jim Mora. "For a guy who's only 215 pounds, he's really strong, too. He can break tackles."

Another two-way threat
New York Jets running back Curtis Martin is another player who excels at both running the ball and catching passes.

Record setter
Running backs aim for the single-season record of 2,105 yards, set in 1984 by Eric Dickerson.

More rumblers

From Red Grange to Steve Van Buren, from Jim Brown to Walter Payton, the parade of great running backs continues through the years.

And the parade continues in today's NFL. Along with Emmitt Smith, Terrell Davis, and Edgerrin James, there are several great runners breaking tackles and landing in end zones every Sunday.

One of them is Marshall Faulk, who helped the St. Louis Rams win Super Bowl XXXIV by combining great running with outstanding receiving.

The former San Diego State and Indianapolis Colts star and four-time Pro Bowl player gained 2,429 yards from scrimmage in 1999, the most ever in a season. Despite missing two games in 2000, Faulk scored 26 times to set an NFL record for most touchdowns in a season.

In Cincinnati, Corey Dillon has put on quite a show in his young NFL career. He rushed for 246 yards in one game as a rookie against Tennessee in 1997.

In 2000, he topped himself, setting an NFL record by rushing for 278 yards in a Bengals' victory over Denver.

Touchdown machine Washington Redskins running back Stephen Davis led the NFL by scoring 17 touchdowns in 1999.

Corey Dillon gained more than 1,000 yards in each of his first four NFL seasons.

Drive the Bus
Jerome (The Bus) Bettis has seven 1,000-yard seasons in his career with the Rams and Steelers.

A different kind of runner is Tennessee's Eddie George. Instead of being small and quick, he is tall and powerful. George, the 1995 Heisman Trophy winner at Ohio State, gained 1,368 yards to earn NFL rookie of the year honors in 1996.

He gained 1,200 or more yards in each of his first five seasons. In 1999, he helped the Titans reach their first Super Bowl. In that game, a loss to St. Louis, George scored 2 second-half touchdowns that helped the Titans tie the score late in the fourth quarter.

Big, strong Eddie George had another 1,000-yard season for Tennessee in 2000.

Whether big, small, fast, slow, tall, short, or none of the above, running backs always play an important role in the success of NFL teams.

How do you get to be a running back? It's simple. Next time you play football, line up behind the quarterback. Then get the ball and run.

Bingo! You're a running back!

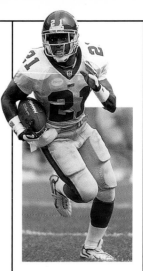

TD Tiki
The Giants' Tiki Barber emerged as a star in 2000. His twin brother Ronde plays for Tampa Bay.

Minnesota's Robert Smith specializes in long scoring runs. He set a club record for rushing yards in 2000.

Glossary

Adversity
Another word for trouble or difficulties that one encounters in life.

Cancer
A type of disease that can strike any part of the body. Caused by cells that mutate in dangerous ways.

Fumble
Occurs when a player with the ball loses control of it on the field by dropping it. Either team can recover the ball.

Lacrosse
A field sport played with sticks that have baskets on one end. Players use the sticks to throw a ball back and forth before throwing it toward a goal.

Line of scrimmage
This is the spot on the field where each play begins. It is set at the point where the previous play ended.

Migraine headache
An especially strong pain in the head, which comes along with blurry vision.

Offensive line
The players who play in front of the quarterback and running backs. Made up of guards, tackles, and a center, the offensive line blocks for runners and passers.

Poll
A kind of vote taken by asking many people the same question or questions.

Quarterback
The key offensive player, he receives the ball to start each play and then hands off to a teammate or passes down the field toward a receiver.

Rookie
A player in his first professional season of a sport.

Running back
Offensive player who lines up behind the quarterback. Responsible for carrying the ball downfield, catching passes, and blocking.

Strategy
The plays a team chooses to run, what players it uses, what formations it sets up, all are part of a team's strategy for success.

Super Bowl
The NFL's championship game, between the champions of the American Football Conference and the National Football Conference.

Touchdown
Scoring play worth six points; scored when a player with the ball crosses the goal line or catches the ball inside the end zone.